Relational Leadership
An Introduction

Leonard Cochran

DEDICATION

To my wife and best friend, Paula and to my awesome
kids Carissa and Jonathan and their families.

CONTENTS

ACKNOWLEDGMENTS

A special thanks goes out to Nancy Pepper for your editing skills. Thank you for your kind words and encouragement too.

Thank you, David Smithey for the quick brainstorming session at Coffee Central. That's proof that one simple conversation can have a greater impact than we might ever imagine. Keep on sharing your wisdom.

CHAPTER ONE

Matt walked out the door of the bakery and pounded on the roof of his car before getting in and sitting down with a huff. "That's one more person that's quit since I've been running this bakery," Matt exclaimed. He knew taking over the bakery wouldn't be easy, but there were so many things he didn't expect. He didn't expect the turnover, nor the drop in sales. In his eyes, nothing had changed, except for him being the new owner and manager.

Matt drove down the road to clear his mind. What was he going to do? He couldn't afford to lose much more business or else he would have to let someone go. Of course, that wasn't an issue right now since he'd had a couple people recently quit. Things just weren't the same since Matt's father passed away. His father trained Matt on how to run the business, but there were so many things that Matt didn't anticipate. It felt like the employees were always needing his attention and that everyone came to him for every single decision. On top of that, sales were dropping, and he couldn't figure out why. There was even an increase in customer complaints. Matt let out a deep sigh and shook his head.

Just as Matt sighed, he noticed a small coffee shop wedged in between a couple retail stores. "The Common Ground," he read out loud as he drove past. He didn't remember seeing it there before. He felt like a little time away from work would do him some good. He decided to turn around and get a cup of coffee and unwind before he returned to work to finish out his day. He parked the car and walked into the small shop.

"Hello," said a voice from the back of the coffee shop. It was a small place. There was a couch against one wall, a few four top tables and some smaller tables for two. It looked more like a large living room instead of the sanitized coffee chain where Matt usually went. "How are you doing today, Dear?" The voice from the back spoke again as an older woman emerged. "I don't think I've seen you here before. My name is Laura. What's your name, Hun?" she asked.

"Hi, my name is Matt. I didn't even know this place existed. For some reason I've never noticed it before." Matt continued to look around the room as his eyes adjusted to the dim lighting. He could see it was clean and just a little "busy" yet somehow it felt very comfortable.

"Well, good to meet you Matt. What can I get for you today?" Laura motioned to the chalkboard with the menu written in colorful chalk with drawings of coffee beans, steaming cups of coffee and a few food items on it. "I don't mean to be rude, but you look like you could use something that will help you relax." Laura continued.

Matt chuckled, "You're not kidding. I don't know if you sell something that strong here. This place looks family friendly." Laura laughed with Matt and responded, "No, we don't sell anything like that here, but I do have a honey lavender tea that's really good. Would you like to give it a try?" "I like my caffeine, but I guess I don't need anything else to help keep me on edge. I'll give it a try." Matt sat at a small counter and watched as Laura prepared his tea.

"So, how long have you been here?" Matt asked. Laura looked over her reading glasses as she prepared his tea. "I opened this up last year after Calvin passed away. He was my husband." She responded. "Oh, I'm sorry for your loss," Matt responded. "You look and sound so calm. So, you started this business on your own?"

"Well Calvin owned a couple of businesses before his passing, and I used to help him out a little. I didn't want to just retire and think about things, so I decided to open this little shop right here to keep myself busy." Laura told Matt.

"Oh, I see. Well, you've got a nice place here. It's a

comfortable feeling place.... I've had my own loss this past year, and I guess that's why I'm under a little stress now. My father ran The Corner Bakery. He was getting ready to retire, so I started working for him about a couple of years before he passed away last year. I don't know what I'm doing differently than him, but it's just not working the same." Matt fumbled through as he tried to explain the current state of the business.

"I'm sorry to hear that Matt. If you don't mind me asking, what's happening in the business now that wasn't happening before?" Laura asked as she handed him his tea. "Who knows? Maybe some of my experience can be of help to you." Matt took a sip of his hot tea. "This is good" he said as he pointed to the tea. "You seem like you're trustworthy, so I don't mind sharing. Just don't tell any of my competitors what I'm about to tell you." Matt gave a small laugh as Laura smiled.

It was strange for Matt to be so open with someone he didn't know, but there was something about Laura that made him feel like he could trust her. Maybe it was the way she wore her glasses on the tip of her nose and looked over them as she spoke. Maybe the lavender in the tea relaxed him more than he thought it would. Regardless of what it was, she was older, and she just might have some wisdom that he could use.

"Well, you see, my dad was a very outgoing guy. Everyone loved him, and he loved everyone. I'm running the business the way he taught me, but the longer I'm running it the worse the business is going. My sales are dropping, and I've had a couple of people quit on me so we're about to be short staffed. I guess if sales keep falling off that won't be an issue. Plus, we have a few employees that act like they just don't want to work anymore. I can't get them motivated to do their work."

"Is there anything else going on that you can think of Matt?" Laura asked. Matt took another drink of his tea and chuckled as he said, "Isn't that enough?" He thought briefly and said, "We have had just a few customer complaints lately about the quality of our products. But nothing too big."

"I have a strange question to ask you; is your personality similar to your father's?" Matt glanced down at the counter and folded his paper napkin. "We're about as different as night and day. He was always bubbly, maybe just a little loud, and he could remember anyone's name after meeting them for the first time. I'm more comfortable with the numbers side of the business. In fact, I used to do the accounting long before I started working in the shop."

"Is it safe to say that the people working for you might be having a hard time adjusting to you being the new leader?" Matt didn't flinch when he responded, "Yes, it's safe to say. Almost every day I hear someone talking about how great my dad was." Laura leaned in and whispered, "You know Matt, you aren't your father. You might be running the business with the same rules, but you're leading it differently than what your father did." Laura looked at Matt as he reflected on what she said. He could see the kindness in her eyes and recognized she wasn't trying to cast judgement on him but she was honestly trying to help him uncover the root cause of why he was struggling to manage the bakery.

Matt slowly responded, "I think you might be right. If I'm honest, I know I've been focused on our sales too much. I just wanted to make the bakery more profitable. My dad was never too worried about profits. He was more interested in the employees and the customers. Don't get me wrong, he made a profit, but not nearly as much as what he could have."

"My husband was an expert relational leader," Laura said without hesitation. "He understood the importance of balance. No disrespect, but from what you're telling me, there's a chance your business is a little out of balance right now." Matt responded. "Balance? What kind of balance? What is relational leadership?" Matt looked at the time on his phone. "I can spare another few minutes before I need to go back to work, but I would like to hear about relational leadership."

"The way that Calvin liked to explain relational leadership was leadership focused on four key areas: Purpose, Principles, People, and Profits." Laura explained. Matt asked, "Do you mind if I take notes?" "Not at all."

So, Matt took out his phone and typed, "Relational leadership is leadership focused on four key areas: Purpose, Principles, People, and Profits"

> *Relational Leadership is leadership focused on four key areas:*
> *Purpose, Principles, People, and Profits.*

Laura continued, "Much like your chair has four legs, if one leg is short, the whole chair is unstable. From what you've said Matt, it sounds like the bakery might be a little out of balance." Matt nodded, "I guess that might be fair to say. Could you explain each of the key areas or 'legs' as you call them? That will help my understanding." Laura gave a great big smile as she responded, "I would love to!"

"Before I break it down, I want to warn you that when you lead this way, the concepts are simple, but it's not easy." Matt interrupted Laura, "what do you mean, 'it's simple, but not easy'?" Matt took out his phone and typed, "It's simple, but not easy".

Laura continued. "It means, the concepts of leading this way are simple or common. In fact, when I talk to some people about all this, they say it's common sense. But when we dig into the work of trying to get things done, it ends up being harder than what we might like. Other times, we think we've found a shortcut, so we might deviate from these concepts in effort to save time, money, or effort. It's too easy to let our guard down and forget why we do things the way we do them." Matt nodded to show his understanding as Laura continued to talk.

Purpose

"The first area I'll address is Purpose. We can establish a purpose as an individual or as a company. Most companies have a mission statement or a vision statement, but even before those are written, someone took time to think about the purpose of the business. Why do we want to go into business? What do we hope to accomplish? As Simon Sinek says, 'it's the why behind our what.' Purpose is what keeps you going in each day, even when people are quitting, and sales are in a slump." Laura said with a slight smile. Matt smiled quickly to confirm his understanding as he typed the word "Purpose" into his phone notes.

"Also, the REASON we do business will impact HOW we do our business. In the same way, the reason you lead will impact how you lead. So, it's important to have a clear understanding of why we're doing what we're doing. If you're just out to make money, you might make money for a while, but in time, customers won't have a compelling reason to come back. Eventually, they'll realize your motives are purely self-serving, and they'll take their business to someone else. Customers, and maybe more importantly, your team members need to understand why you're in business. Your team members will appreciate that you're trying to accomplish something greater than just serving your own needs, but that you're somehow contributing to the greater community."

> *The reason you lead will impact how you lead.*

Matt continued to type notes from time to time as Laura continued to speak. "So, having a higher purpose is the first area of Relational Leadership. Then, I like to put Principles right after Purpose. Does all this make sense so far, Matt?" She asked. "Yes, it does. I know that I'm going to have to think about the Purpose of my bakery. My dad started the business before I was even born. So, it's just been there. I never did ask him why he was doing it for a business."

"You might just have to evaluate why YOU are still keeping the business going then." Matt acknowledged that Laura was right and then he asked, "You said you like to put Principles after Purpose, why is that?"

Principles

"That's a good question Matt. Let me explain what I mean by Principles and as I do, I think you will understand why they are in that order," Laura responded.

"When I reference principles, I'm talking about the ethics or values that motivates the work that you do. So, if you think of your Purpose as your 'why' then you might think of your principles as your 'how". You can even think of your principles as the moral compass of how you pursue your purpose. You need to define them to keep you on the right path."

> *Principles are the moral compass*
> *of how you pursue your purpose.*

"So," Matt said, "if I were on a sports team, and our sole purpose was to win games at all costs, my principles might allow me to bend or even break the rules if that will help me win the game?" Both Matt and Laura smiled as she responded. "You might technically be right on that one, but let's hope the team would have a higher purpose than just winning; especially winning at any cost." They both laughed.

"A lot of large companies create values to clarify their operating principles. They have nice posters and talk about them frequently to ensure the team members understand how they should be conducting business." Laura went on to explain, "For my little coffee shop here, one of my principles is 'integrity,' so, I'm committed to always operate with integrity. Even if it costs me money."

"How can operating with integrity cost you money?" Matt asked. "It could be as simple as the one time our coffee vendor delivered more than what I had ordered, and they didn't bill me for it. I could have kept it and not told them. Those few pounds of coffee beans could have made a lot of brewed coffee that I could have sold and made a lot of profit since I didn't pay for the beans. But I called the vendor and let them know the shipment was wrong. So, it cost me a few dollars in sales."

"Hmm, it was their mistake, I'm not sure I would have said anything," Matt reflected out loud. "Oh, it crossed my mind," Laura admitted. "But they learned that they could trust me because of that. I'm not sure how much that's worth in dollars and cents, but it sure helps me sleep better at night. Also, that one conversation helped to strengthen our relationship. For example, one time they had a lot of orders for a particular type of coffee beans, and they didn't have enough inventory to fill all their customer orders, so, they made sure I got my full order when others didn't. I'm really sure it's because they respect the fact that I was honest with them. That leads me to the third area of Relational Leadership; people."

People

"It's called Relational Leadership, because of the people. You can't have relationships without people. So, even though this is the third area, it's by no means the least important. As I said, if your chair has one short leg it's not as stable as it needs to be, so all four of these areas are important. You can't even have a business without people." Laura smiled.

"A Relational Leader should consider at least four groups of people when making decisions. The groups are team members, customers, vendors, and ourselves. There might be more, but these four are the ones that you likely have the greatest impact on. These are the people that you have the biggest relationship with as a business."

"First, and foremost are your team members; they are the most important group of people you should focus on. They are your most important asset. Most team members spend more of their waking hours at work than they do at home. So, you can see how the purpose of your business and the principles of your business impact the people in your business. They live, eat and breathe it almost as much as you!" Matt didn't say a word as he gave a simple, "hmm" sound and intently listened.

> *Team members are*
> *your most important asset.*

"One of the characteristics of a relational leader is a desire to serve their team members so they can grow. I don't want to have someone doing the same job five years from now unless that's the job they want to be doing. If they want to advance, I want to do what I can do to see them advance. Sometimes that means even growing them to the point that I can't afford them. I'm a small business owner, and I can't promote everyone, but I can give them skills that are transferable to other places IF they choose to leave."

"You mean you deliberately train your employees knowing they're going to quit?" Matt asked. "I wouldn't think of it like that Matt," Laura responded. "If someone is doing a good job, and they want to grow, I'm going to help them. I've had some team members decide to leave because they wanted more than what this little shop has to offer. I've had others say that this place felt too much like a family and they didn't want to go to work for anyone else.

Even if their title and the pay was better someplace else, they have chosen to stay. Don't forget Matt, money will only keep people for so long. Everyone wants to be seen, heard, and loved. They're going to go where they can get that, or they'll go with the intention of making so much money they can quit later and then be around someone that can see, hear, and love them." She said with a little laugh.

"I make it a point of getting to know my team members. I learn about their families, hobbies, and everything that I would find out about a friend. If we're going to spend so much time together, we might as well get to know each other and enjoy each other's company."

"I guess that makes sence," Matt said. "I just figured we were at work to get things done, and we'll enjoy our time afterwards." Laura looked at Matt and asked, "So, how's that working for you?" Matt's shoulders slumped ever so slightly. "I guess not too well," he said, as he reflected on his recent turnover.

"I've found over the years that when I take care of my team members, they do a much better job taking care of our customers. But that doesn't mean we can ignore our customers. We're here to meet their needs too. Most of us easily understand the importance of our customers, so I won't spend time on that. I've also shared an example of the relationship I have with my coffee vendor, so you can see the importance of that too. I want to hit on the last group of people; ourselves."

"I was going to ask you about that." Matt responded. Laura continued, "As a leader of any kind, it's also important for us to think about ourselves from time to time. We certainly want to serve our team members and serve our communities, but every decision we make directly impacts us. We're either delegating it and following up, or we're doing it ourselves. So, we need to ensure we're making healthy decisions. Have you ever overcommitted yourself?"

"Ha, yes," Matt said, "more than once. I keep telling myself, I'll never do that again. Then I do it again."

"Well, Matt, as a good leader, we have to be responsible for our own mental and physical well-being. Sometimes that means NOT committing to do *good* things, because we need to do what is *best* for ourselves. I get it, it sounds selfish, but no one is going to take better care of us than we take care of ourselves. So sometimes we have to make unpopular decisions and stick to them as a matter of principle." Matt gave a small smile and couldn't help but notice how each of the areas of relational leadership seemed to connect with each other.

Profits

"The last area that relational leaders focus on is profits. Clearly if we don't make a profit in business, we won't stay in business. We want to operate efficiently, so we can earn a fair profit. It's not our sole purpose. But that takes planning on the front end. It also takes maintenance along the way. If the needs of the people we serve changes, then we might need to make the investment of our time, talent, and treasure to adjust our strategy and maybe even how we do business, so we can continue to be profitable."

> *We want to operate efficiently,*
> *so we can earn a fair profit.*

"Now, I know in some big companies they have to worry about shareholders and keeping them happy. But, hopefully, if the shareholders can be educated to know something will be profitable in the longer term, they'll be more forgiving in the present."

"I guess the thing to remember about profits as a relational leader is to know that profits aren't a bad thing. Some people think they are, and I'm not about to debate that. In fact, I'm no economic professor, you can take a class on that if you want, but what I will say is I've pre-determined how much of a profit I would like for my business to be able to reinvest back into the business and to put some into other investments. That's all I'll say about that."

Matt looked at his notes and then looked at the time. "Oh my goodness," he said. "It looks like I've been away from the bakery longer than I intended to be! I better head back now. I do have one question for you Laura" He said with a pause, "these four areas of relational leadership sound great, but where do I begin?"

"Well, it starts with a conversation or two, but we'll need to pick that up the next time we meet," responded Laura. "We will meet again... won't we?" Laura asked.

"You've given me no choice," Matt said with a laugh. "I know I need to clarify my purpose. That might help me with my principles. I know I need to work on my people and on my profits. So far, I've got a lot of areas to work on." Matt confessed.

"Just review all four of key areas and focus on the first two areas for now, and we can talk strategy next time." Laura encouraged him.

Matt left the coffee shop and as he entered his car to return to The Corner Bakery, he reflected on the conversation he just had with his new connection, Laura. He could sense there was a lot of hard work ahead, but also he had a sense of hope. Somehow, he knew this one conversation was going to change his future.

Chapter One Reflection Questions

1. Anyone can be Relational Leader regardless of their job title. Are you a Relational Leader? Why or why not?

2. Reflect on the four key areas of Relational Leadership: Purpose, Principles, People and

Profits. Which area needs your attention immediately?

3. It looks like Laura has become Matt's Relational Leadership coach. Do you have a coach to help guide you on your journey?

4. Have you defined your personal Purpose, and your personal Principles? If you have not, take time to define them now.

_____

_____

_____

_____

_____

_____

_____

_____

_____

_____

_____

_____

_____

_____

_____

_____

_____

_____

_____

_____

_____

_____

_____

_____

_____

_____

_____

_____

_____

_____

_____

_____

_____

_____

_____

_____

_____

_____

_____

_____

CHAPTER TWO

Matt returned to The Corner Bakery at closing time. Fortunately, Nicole was working, so Matt knew everything would be fine. Nicole had been working at the bakery for a number of years. She started when Matt was a teenager. His dad always told Matt, "One day you need to marry a girl like Nicole when you get old enough. She's got a good head on her shoulders and she's a good hard worker. Dependable people like her are worth their weight in gold."

"Hi Nicole. I'm sorry that I'm so late getting back. I needed a moment to breathe so I went and had a cup of coffee. I met the nicest lady." Nicole looked up from behind the counter with a smirk on her face. "Everything went fine, Matt. Thanks for asking," she said sarcastically. Nicole continued to remove the sheet pans of donuts from the display case.

"Oh, I'm sorry Nicole. I've just been so preoccupied with Emma quitting this morning and our sales being down. I don't know how my dad handled all this pressure." Matt paused, "How was your afternoon, Nicole? How did things go?"

"Matt, you know everything went fine. I'm not going to let anything happen if you're gone, and I'm here. You don't have to worry about me. So, you said you met the nicest lady; tell me about it," Nicole requested.

"We talked about a lot of things," Matt responded. He washed and dried his hands at the small sink behind the counter. He put on a pair of clear plastic gloves as he spoke, "Her name was Laura. Apparently, her husband used to be a businessman before he passed away. She could tell that I was frustrated, so I kind of dumped on her about my dad passing away and how I've been struggling to handle things at the bakery since I've taken over."

"I'm listening," Nicole said. "I just want to get out of here sometime tonight, so I'm going to keep consolidating these donuts on as few trays as possible as we talk. Matt held up his hands with the oversized clear gloves on his hands; "I put these lovely gloves on so I could help." Matt said. "I'll try and move my hands as much as I move my mouth," he said with a big smile on his face.

"Anyhow," Matt continued, "Laura explained a type of leadership called Relational Leadership." He took off his gloves and pulled up the notes on his phone and continued, "She said, 'Relational Leadership is leadership focused on four areas: Purpose, Principles, People and Profits.' My homework assignment is to review each of these four areas in this business and to focus on the first two areas for now."

"I know the first thing that I need to do is dig into the purpose of this business," he said as he placed the gloves back on his hands and continued working. "I'm not sure why my dad started this business. If I can't figure it out, then I need to take ownership of our purpose moving forward." Nicole moved the empty sheet pans to the back of the bakery and put them in a stack of sheet pans that needed to be washed. "What do you mean, purpose?" She asked.

Matt picked up a tray of donuts and followed Nicole to the back of the bakery. He covered the tray with plastic wrap as he spoke. "The purpose of any business needs to be bigger than just making money. Our purpose needs to somehow be bigger than just our shop. It answers the question of why we do what we do. You know, like 'how are we making the world a better place?' type of a question. You've worked here for almost as long as I can remember, do you know what my dad's purpose was in all this?" He made a gesture with his hands as he asked.

"Matt, I'm not sure what his grand logic was for this little bakery. I just know that your dad loved people and loved to make people happy. He was good at it, too." Nicole stated. "I know," Matt said. "Everyone likes to keep reminding me of that fact."

Matt counted the money from the register. He gave a sigh as he reviewed the sales for the day. "You know Nicole, our sales have been off for the past four months. Last year, we did a lot better than we're doing now." Matt paused and looked up, "Can I asked ask you a serious question, Nicole?"

Nicole was busy doing the final walk through of the bakery to ensure everything was ready for the opening crew in the morning. She could hear the strain in Matt's voice as he spoke. She paused, to give Matt her full attention. "Sure, Matt. What's your question?"

"What am I doing differently than my dad did when he ran the bakery?" As Matt asked, Nicole could see the pain in his eyes. She knew that he was doing the best that he could to keep the bakery going and to make it a success. She quietly took a deep breath before she responded. "Aww, Matt. You're doing the best you can." Matt glanced at her, and she knew he was looking for more than just her sympathy. "You know how everyone goes on about how your dad loved people?" Nicole asked.

"Yeah, I know," Matt responded. "Well," Nicole continued as she tried to be truthful and kind at the same time. She had known Matt longer than anyone else that worked in the bakery, so she figured if anyone was going to be honest with him, it would be her. "I think sometimes, the team feels like you're more interested in the numbers of the business than you are the people who work for the business." She almost held her breath after the last words left her mouth.

Matt looked down as he struggled to think of what to say next. He had suspected exactly what Nicole had vocalized, but he had hoped he was wrong. "I care. I'm just not my dad. I don't show that I care the same way that he did." After a brief pause, Matt followed up with another question, "What do you think I should do about it, Nicole? You know that I care about everyone."

"I don't expect anyone wants you to behave like your dad, but there are some simple things you could do to help improve their perception and to show them you care." Nicole looked at the time. It was getting late. She realized this was not going to be settled in one simple conversation. "It will take some time but start by talking to the team about things other than work. Talk to them about their families and what's going on in their lives. Heck, talk about what's going on in your life."

"That brings me full circle back to relational leadership," Matt said. "Laura was reminding me this morning that we spend more of our awake time at work than any other place, so we may as well enjoy it. It makes sense that what happens at home is going to affect everyone's work when they get here, so I guess I don't need to ignore it."

Nicole could see that Matt had received her suggestion with an open mind, so she thought she would make one more suggestion before the opportunity passed, "You may also request a little more input from the team; especially the younger team members. They want to have their voices heard." Matt looked up. "The younger team members have been here the shortest time. Do you think they would have any worthwhile suggestions?" There was a pause, and then Matt spoke again, "I didn't mean that to sound like that, but honestly, what could they have to contribute?"

Nicole responded, "You asked for my thoughts, and I'm just throwing you a couple of ideas, Matt." He sighed, "The voice of reason... You're right; I did ask. Thank you. I don't mean to sound defensive. I need some time to process this," Matt continued. "Let's call it a night, and I'll give it some more thought. You know me, my mind is more like a slow cooker than a microwave," Matt said with a laugh. Nicole smiled and tried to assure Matt that she knew he would get the bakery back up and going before too long.

As they walked out the door and Matt locked it behind them, he thanked Nicole for her honesty and for her support. "Just be yourself, Matt, and be human. You're a person running a business, you're not a machine, and the team that works for you are people, too. How hard can it be?" Nicole said with a big smile. "Good night," Matt replied with a small smile.

The next day Matt was reflecting on all that had happened the day prior. He felt that it was not a coincidence that he had met Laura and that Nicole had shared so openly with him. He loved running The Corner Bakery, and he loved all of the team members. As he reflected, he realized "I'm in it for the people!" Matt said out loud to himself. "That's it! My purpose is for people! I know that's not specific enough, but it's a starting point." Matt took out a large yellow legal pad of paper and grabbed a pen so he could write down his thoughts and see them.

At the top of the page, Matt wrote, "Purpose = people." His mind went back to when he was about ten years of age, and his dad had just opened the bakery. In his mind, he could see his dad greeting everyone that came in the door. The Corner Bakery was the first family-owned bakery to open in the community in several years. People flooded in for weeks, and business was booming. He thought about the time his dad used money from the bakery to help the Henderson family when the home they were renting burned down. His dad found out they didn't have rental insurance, so he gave them a big "loan" and told them to pay it back whenever they could. Even at that young age, Matt knew his dad wasn't expecting to see the money again. That's just how his dad was.

There were times the bakery nearly went broke because

of his dad's generosity. "I guess that's why I became the numbers guy," Matt spoke aloud to himself again. "I didn't want to see dad lose his business because of his love of people," he said with a whisper. Matt took the pen and wrote, "give back responsibly" on the legal pad.

"Laura told me that a good purpose has to be bigger than just us; it should be something to help the community," Matt thought to himself. "Giving back is one way, but there has to be more…" Suddenly Matt realized, he kept seeing smiling faces as he thought back to when his dad was running the bakery. Again, he picked up the yellow pad and this time he wrote, "create happiness". Matt thought for a moment and wrote on the paper one more time. This time he wrote in larger print than the times before, "WE WANT TO MAKE THE WORLD HAPPY BY GIVING MOMENTS OF JOY".

Was that it? Was that the purpose of the bakery? Matt knew that he had captured the vision his father had. In his excitement, Matt grabbed the notepad and pen as he headed out the door. He felt he had to share this with his new connection at the Common Ground coffee shop.

"Hi Laura," Matt exclaimed as he entered the door of the coffee shop. Laura was working at the counter as he entered. "Hey there, friend," Laura said. "How are you doing today, Matt?" She asked. "I think I may have found my purpose. Or, I mean, I think I may have found the purpose of my business," Matt excitedly responded.

"Well, you timed it right again, I've got some time to chat. Tell me what you've got." Laura responded. "I want to order a large, iced mocha coffee with a shot of mint first, and then I would be thrilled if you would join me in a conversation."

Matt paid for his coffee, and once it was prepared, he motioned to Laura that they could sit at the small table with two chairs. She nodded and followed him over to the table after fixing herself a cup of hot coffee. Matt pulled out his legal pad with notes and sat it in front of himself in the middle of the table.

"What have you come up with, Matt?" Laura asked. "I've been working on the first leg of relational leadership. I've been working on the purpose of the business. It just sort of hit me, and I wrote it down. I think it's a good fit, but I wanted to see what you thought about it… How does this sound? We want to make the world happy by giving moments of joy." He almost held his breath as he waited for Laura's response.

"I like it!" She said with enthusiasm. "It's bigger than just you. It encompasses the community and beyond, so it's a lofty vision. That's really good, Matt." Laura continued to explain, "The most important thing, however, is it needs to be something that YOU believe in. If you believe in it, you'll be able to find others who will follow you towards working for that purpose."

"That's where I get a little nervous," he admitted. "I'm not a good people person like my dad was, so I don't know if people will want to follow me like they did him." Laura looked at Matt with understanding eyes and without judgement, and then she said, "Matt, you aren't your dad, so you'll have to find your own way. People will follow you because of your purpose, not just your personality. The way YOU do it might look different than the way someone else would do it, and that's okay. You'll be able to reach different people because of your differences." Matt's expression still looked like he wasn't sure, so Laura continued. "You may not think you're good at leading, but don't let that stop you. Use any doubt that you have in yourself to keep you humble. Don't ever give up because of doubt. Besides, you've got your team to help you." Laura finished.

"I guess that makes sense," he responded. "Oh, and you'll get better as time progresses," Laura assured him. "No one can do it on their own. There's an ancient saying, 'one can put a thousand to flight, and two can put ten thousand to flight.' That means, when you work with a team of people towards a single purpose, you'll accomplish a whole lot more than you ever could on your own. So, you're just going to have to trust your team to help."

Matt laughed, "I think that's another area that I need to work on." Laura smiled, "No one said relational leadership was easy, did they?" They both chuckled and continued to drink their coffee as the conversation continued. "I don't want to take up too much of your time, Laura, after all, I know you have a business to run." Matt said. "Oh, I don't mind it at all Matt. You remind me a little of my son, so I guess you can just think of this as my way of giving back to a younger generation," Laura said.

"I don't think of myself as too young anymore," Matt responded, "the kids now days that I'm hiring aren't anything like what they used to be." Laura laughed, "You, making that statement, PROVES you're getting a little older," she said with a big smile. He gave a little chuckle, "I guess you got me that time."

"Well, congratulations on defining your purpose, Matt. I know that was no easy task. You would be amazed at how many companies and organizations never clearly define their purpose," Laura said. "Keep in mind, your defined purpose is your 'North Star' or your 'True North'. You'll want to look at all you do and confirm it is in alignment with your purpose."

Chapter Two Reflection Questions
1. In the first chapter of this book, you were asked to write a purpose. After reading chapter two, take time to reflect on your purpose and verify that it's big and bold enough. Take the time to make any needed revisions.

2. As relational leaders, we need to leverage the strengths of our team members. It's good to understand our own strengths and weaknesses first. Take time to honestly assess yourself. What areas can you use the most help?

3. Who can help you in your areas of weakness?

4. What areas do you feel the most confident?

_____

_____

_____

_____

_____

_____

_____

_____

_____

_____

_____

_____

_____

_____

_____

CHAPTER THREE

"So, I've written the purpose for the bakery, what's the next step? From the notes on my phone, it looks like I need to define some principles," Matt said answering his own question. "That's right," said Laura. "You'll want to find three to five words that characterize HOW you will 'make the world happy by giving moments of joy'. "What does that look like?" Matt asked with a puzzled expression.

"Let's briefly go back to your purpose statement again. On a practical level, what can you, as an organization or even as an individual, do to make the world happy? What can you do to create moments of joy?" Laura asked. Matt explained, "Part of how I came up with this purpose was thinking about how my father always made people smile. Heck, people smile when they see fresh donuts being put in the case. They smile when they bite into their favorite doughnut. I also thought about how my father helped people, and they would smile in gratitude for his help. Those are some of the things that made me think of this as a purpose."

"That's beautiful, Matt," Laura responded. "For the next step, I want you to think of some words to express the ethics or values that will guide you in accomplishing the purpose you've just described. You used the word 'smile' and you talked about your dad giving back. You can use a phrase if you must, but it's easier to remember a few short words. And remember, this needs to fit you and your company. You'll want your team members to be able to recite these principles back to you once you've established them."

"I think it would be easiest for you to create a big list of words; just brainstorm ideas, and then narrow it down," Laura continued. "You may want to collaborate with someone for some ideas. It's your purpose, so these should be your principles once it's all said and done," Laura said encouraging him.

"It sounds like I've got my next homework assignment," Matt said. "I'll need to take some time to think this over." Laura nodded, "Yes, take your time. You can adjust them in the future if you need, but it's best if you can land on the right ones the first time around."

"Can I share them with you when I get my list completed?" Matt asked. "You know you better share it with me if you know what's good for you," Laura said with a laugh. "Once you've got it narrowed down, or almost got it completed, share your list with a few people that have insight into you and your business and who are willing to be truthful with you."

Matt left the coffee shop, and for the next several days he would add a word to the list he kept on his phone. At the top of the list, he had his new found purpose, and a listing of words underneath. Sometimes he listed similar words knowing he would narrow his selection later. For example, he listed both "giving" and "generous" as he thought about how much his dad had contributed to the neighborhood.

Matt included several words he liked, even when he wasn't sure if they would make the final cut or not. The list included, "honest, helpful, giving, generous, happy, smiling, and financially responsible." He knew that once the list was close to completion, he would share it with Nicole. She understood the business and Matt better than anyone else he could think of. He knew she would be a great person to review his list.

After a few more days, Matt was feeling comfortable with the list he had made. A few items were removed, and his most solid choices remained. For a moment, it looked like he could form an acrostic with the list. "Ugh!" He exclaimed. "I've looked at this so long, it's all starting to run together." Matt went to the bakery and offered to treat

Nicole to lunch if she would provide her feedback on the principles he had selected so far.

Matt took Nicole to a small Mexican restaurant toward the edge of town. Everyone knew them for their fresh hot chips and their cheese dip. Matt and Nicole were able to be seated as soon as they arrived. "Let's eat first, and we'll talk business afterwards," Matt suggested.

After a short lunch, Matt showed his list to Nicole. "What do you think?" Nicole slowly reviewed the list and reflected on the purpose statement that was at the top of the listing. "I thought you were supposed to narrow this list down to about four or five words," Nicole responded. "I know, but it just reached the point that I couldn't edit it anymore. That's why I wanted to review it with you," he said with a cheerful tone and a smile.

Nicole asked Matt to explain why he had selected the words that were on his list. She listened intently as he explained each selection. After he finished explaining, she made an observation, "Most of the words you selected start with the letter C. It would be neat if they all did. It would make the list more memorable."

"They don't have to start with the same letter... but to your point, it would make it easier to remember them. Do you have any thoughts, Nicole?" Just as Nicole was about to speak, Matt's cellphone rang. "Go ahead," Nicole said as Matt looked at the number of the caller on his phone. He pulled the phone back and looked a little shocked, so

Nicole figured it must have been important.

"Hello," Matt said as he answered the phone. "Yes, this is he…. Yes… excuse me? … what time did it happen? …. I see…. How bad is it? … oh my … I'll be there within thirty minutes." Matt hung up the phone and put it in his pocket. "I'm sorry, Nicole, I need to go. My elderly neighbor just fell and broke her hip. She has me listed as a family contact since her children live so far away. She's at the hospital, and it sounds like she's just a little shaken up. I had better go!"

Matt rushed out the door of the restaurant and left Nicole sitting there holding his pad of paper. Nicole was a little startled to see Matt respond so quickly. She had little exposure to him outside of work, so she certainly didn't realize that he was the emergency contact for his neighbor. The only thing Nicole knew about Matt's personal life was that he was married and had a couple of children who were young adults. If it weren't for her attending his father's funeral, she might not even know that much.

Nicole picked up the pad of paper and began to leave. She recognized because of the current situation; she was going to see some of Matt's personal principles lived out right before her eyes. She left the restaurant and went home after running a couple of errands.

Several hours later Nicole received a call from Matt. He apologized for abruptly leaving their lunch meeting and explained the situation about his neighbor to her again. She patiently listened to him explain the same thing he had said to her prior to leaving the restaurant so quickly. "So, how is your neighbor doing?" She asked. "She was pretty shaken up," Matt responded. "She had heard a noise at her front door and went to see what it was. I guess she stumbled and ended up falling off her porch when she was investigating the noise. If it weren't for someone passing by, she might still be laying out in her yard."

"That sounds serious, Matt," Nicole responded. "It is. She's still needing some help," Matt responded. "I'm wanting to help her. Her recovery is going to take quite a while due to her health. So, I want to see what we can do to help remodel her home to accommodate a wheelchair. That type of thing isn't going to be covered by her insurance."

"That sounds like that might be a bit of an undertaking for someone who doesn't know construction. Do you think you're up for that, Matt?" Nicole asked. "Oh, I'm not going to do the work, I'm going to use my financial skills to oversee the project while someone else does the work." Matt responded with a laugh. "I might also promote it at the bakery; 'buy a dozen doughnuts and 25% of the cost goes to a cause or something like that."

Nicole hadn't seen Matt so engaged in anything so quickly as he was interested in this construction project. She was amazed as he jumped into action to help his neighbor. It was a side of him that she hadn't seen before. She wanted to ask him about the principles list that they had been working on, but she could discern that it wasn't a priority right now. Nicole glanced at the list again, and with a slight smile on her face, she added the word "compassionate" to the list.

Over the next several days, Matt wasn't around the bakery as much as usual. His hospital visits and the project he was working on for his neighbor consumed a fair amount of his time. He had to entrust Nicole to handle more of the daily operation of the bakery than he had in the past. She was grateful for his trust, and she almost felt a new sense of energy when she arrived at work. She enjoyed having the added responsibilities.

After several days Matt's schedule slowed down. He remembered his conversations with Laura, and then he remembered the list of principles that he had left with Nicole. "I guess I had better get my list of principles finalized." He said to himself. He called Nicole and offered her a cup of coffee for their follow-up conversation. It was set. He would meet her at The Common Ground coffee shop.

"Hey, Nicole," Matt called out from back of the coffee shop near the register. "Thanks for coming out and helping me finalize the principles list that I had started. Let me order you something before we get started." Nicole walked over to him. "Hey, Matt. Thanks, I'll just have a hot Chai

Tea," Nicole responded. Matt placed the order and sat with Nicole at one of the small tables with two chairs. He looked around for Laura, and it didn't appear that she was working.

"I don't see my friend Laura, so you might not get to meet her today. Maybe you can meet her another time," Matt said to Nicole. "That would be nice," She responded. "Well, Nicole, what did you think about the list of principles?" Matt asked.

Nicole placed the notepad on the table so both of them were able to read the list. The purpose was written at the top of the pad with the listing of principles beneath: "WE WANT TO MAKE THE WORLD HAPPY BY GIVING MOMENTS OF JOY. Kind, caring, giving, cheerful, resourceful, committed, compassionate."

"What did you think about it?" Matt asked. "I like it really well," she responded. "I noticed several of the words started with the letter 'C'. I thought it might be neat if all the words started with the same letter. Oh, I added the word compassionate when I saw how you responded to your neighbor who broke her hip. That seemed like a good word to add."

Matt looked over the listing in deep thought. "I like that you added the word compassionate. Maybe that could replace 'giving' and 'caring' since the list needs to be consolidated. The word 'resourceful' doesn't fit in very well. I wonder if there's an alternative for it," Matt said. Nicole searched for a synonym for the word "resourceful". "Look Matt, one of the synonyms is 'clever'. What do you think about that?" Matt chucked as he thought about it. They continued to discuss the words and their meaning for a few minutes before pausing.

"This might not be too bad," he said. Matt updated the paper and let out a laugh. I like this. I know 'kind' doesn't start with the letter 'c' but, I like it." Matt showed Nicole the updated paper: "WE WANT TO MAKE THE WORLD HAPPY BY GIVING MOMENTS OF JOY. Kind, compassionate, cheerful, clever."

Both Matt and Nicole looked at the paper with smiles on their faces and sat silently for just a moment. "I think that's the final version," Matt said breaking the silence. Just as he spoke, he saw Laura entering the coffee shop. "Well, look who is here. It's Laura!" Matt called out and invited her to join them at their table.

"I don't have time for too much conversation today, but I'll be glad to meet your friend, and you can show me what you've been working on," Laura responded pointing to the pad of paper. "This is Nicole. She worked for my father at his bakery before I started there. She's been such a great help. I've told her what you shared about relational leadership. She's seen the new purpose that I've written, and she's been helping me define the principles that will guide us as we work towards that purpose. That's what we have here." Matt handed Laura the notepad with the vision and final listing of principles.

Laura looked over the list and smiled. "You've talked it through and defined what these principles mean to you?" Laura asked. "Oh yes. Nicole and I have been hammering away at this for a few days now," Matt responded. "That's good. I know I've emphasized it several times, but I can't stress it enough; you want to make this list your own," Laura said.

"Not a problem at all. The further I dig into relational leadership, the more it makes sense to me. I'm excited about sharing our new purpose and principles with everyone at the bakery," Matt said with eagerness in his voice. "Well, the next area of focus is 'people'. So, you're in a good position to begin thinking about how you will announce it to people," Laura said as she looked over her glasses with a smile.

"Let me see, the people are my employees, customers, vendors and myself," Matt said. "Is that right?" Laura nodded, "Could I make a suggestion? You may consider calling your employees 'team members'. I know it might be a subtle difference, but it just might make them feel like they can contribute more than some hired hands," she said with laugh. "That's a simple fix. From now on, I'll call them team members!" Matt said in a determined voice.

"That sounds good, Matt. It was so good seeing you

again. Nicole, it was such a pleasure meeting you. You keep this young man in line, okay?" Laura reached and gave each of them a hug as they exchanged their goodbyes. She hustled into the back for a quick moment and returned, heading to the exit doors with the book she had stopped in to pick up. She waved at them both as she left.

Chapter Three Reflection Questions

1. Principles can be used as a compass of how you pursue your purpose. Make a listing of the three to five primary principles of your organization.
2. Review your principles and define any words for clarity.
3. Review your listing again; What can be done to make it more meaningful and memorable to others?
4. Confirm that your purpose and principles describe your organization accurately.

_____

_____

_____

_____

_____

_____

_____

_____

CHAPTER FOUR

Matt was feeling good about the fact he had finalized the new purpose and the principles for the bakery. Putting in the effort to do that made him feel a little more enthusiastic about his work. It didn't alleviate the pressure of the heavy workload from being short team members but somehow, he felt more optimistic. Somehow, he believed the future of the bakery just might be brighter than what he had envisioned it just a couple of short weeks ago.

One of the last things that Laura had said to Matt was still bouncing in his head. She had suggested that he call his employees "team members". Changing the wording wouldn't be difficult, but Matt was pondering the distinction she had pointed out, "so they don't feel like hired hands." He had to admit that being a "team member" sounded more empowering than being an "employee." When a person is part of a team, it implies participation and engagement. The word 'Employee' implies that a person is there for the money. Of course, they needed the money, but to reach the new purpose of the bakery, it might require a shift in their attitudes, and that included Matt's as well.

Matt decided that since the bakery had 12 team members, he would take the time to talk to everyone individually, rather than have a team meeting to announce the purpose and principles. This would be a good way for him to build some much-needed relationships with the team. He also realized how much of a contribution Nicole had been in helping him since he took over, and especially as he was helping his neighbor and working on the new purpose and principles, so he decided it was time to offer her a promotion from Shift Leader to Assistant Manager.

"Hey, Nicole," Matt said as he walked into the bakery to begin his workday. "How have things been so far this morning?" He asked. "So far everything has gone smoothly, Matt," Nicole replied. "I want to talk to you for a few minutes when you have the time," Matt motioned towards the office in the back of the bakery. "Okay, let me be sure that we've got enough coffee made, and I'll be right back," Nicole responded.

"What's up, Matt?" Nicole asked as she stood in the door of Matt's office. He offered a seat on the small folding chair that was across from his desk which nearly filled the office. "Nicole, I've been thinking about the work that you do here, and I wanted to promote you to be the new Assistant Manager," Matt said with a big smile. "That would be awesome!" Nicole responded. "You'll have to let me know what your expectations are since it's a new position."

They talked for some time, and Matt explained how important her work was to the bakery. He shared how much he appreciated her honesty in explaining what she had seen in the workplace, and he even expressed how much he enjoyed working with her as a friend. Nicole beamed with a glowing smile. She was happy about the pay increase as well. It had been a couple of years since she had an increase. She had known she was the top earner in the bakery but felt earning more wouldn't be out of order. She was right.

After talking to Nicole, Matt scheduled a time to talk with each of the other team members. One by one he met with them. He shared the new purpose and principles and did his best to just listen. He knew that he was more comfortable with numbers and sometimes got lost in the task of doing work, but he realized his team members were like his family. That was something he hadn't given much thought to in the past.

Matt's team was genuinely pleased that he had spent the time talking with them. It took him a couple of weeks to get to everyone, but he felt it was worth the effort. Matt noticed a pattern from his conversations with them. He had been just a little too controlling and making too many decisions without asking for their feedback first. Nicole had already told him, and it may have been difficult to hear, but it was affirming to know it was true.

Matt laughed out loud, "Well, I guess I must be slow. I just realized; I've spent more time focusing on people than I have since I took over the bakery. I think Laura would be proud," he said. After a brief pause, he said quietly, "I guess my dad would be proud too."

As Matt reflected on his team, and his conversations with them, he realized he needed to make some changes to help increase communication with the team. "Even small operations can improve their efficiency," he said to himself. He wanted to empower the team members more. Some of that would be accomplished by creating some new positions like Nicole's promotion. Some improvements could happen by hearing the voices of the team members more often.

Matt decided that each team member should meet with their team leaders on a regular basis. Each team leader would then meet with their leadership regularly, as well. This would give everyone a chance to be heard. The new structure would allow a chance for more collaboration and problem solving when situations arise.

As these changes were implemented, Matt noticed that the morale of the team seemed to be improving. He remembered what Laura had told him, "Everyone wants to be seen, heard, and loved." With a slight smile on his face, he looked at the notes from his first conversation with Laura and read, "Team members are your most important asset."

There was a subtle shift happening at The Corner Bakery, and it was a good one. As the team members began to feel like they were being heard and loved, Matt noticed the productivity was increasing. Even the quality of work was improving. The team members were being more proactive to avoid product outages. It didn't happen all at once, but it was just a small, subtle shift.

After this shift took place, it spilled over to the customer experience, too. Matt realized there was a correlation between team member satisfaction and customer satisfaction. When the team members were happier, the customers seemed happier, too. Matt felt that the true depth of relational leadership was beginning to sink in. "It really does work," he muttered under his breath with a slight smile.

> *There is a correlation between team member satisfaction and customer satisfaction.*

Matt took out his phone and reviewed the notes from his first meeting with Laura. He read, "A relational leader should consider at least four groups of people when making decisions. The groups are team members, customers, vendors and ourselves." It was clear that things were changing with the team members and ultimately the customers, too. The team members were making the effort to be more friendly as they waited on the customers.

As Matt thought about ways to express gratitude to the bakery customers, he had the idea to roll out a loyalty program for customers who shopped at the bakery frequently. Matt collaborated with the team to design a promotion that would allow the customers to earn points based on their spending. The points could then be used to make purchases from the bakery. After several days of planning, he reached out to a local marketing firm for help naming the program and creating marketing materials. "Never in the history of this bakery have we done anything like this," Matt said proudly.

He wanted to implement the program as quickly as possible in hopes of growing the business. The marketing would also reach prospective customers, so maybe that would enlarge their customer base. Matt and the team were excited about the program and shared the information with every customer.

Matt had been so busy with all the new changes. He had almost forgotten the notes on his phone. He had taken his phone out to make a notation and saw the last note opened was called 'Relational Leadership'. That reminded him that he still had some work to do. He hadn't completed all four of the areas of focus. In fact, he hadn't finished reviewing all the areas of focusing on people!

He felt like there were improvements made for the team members and for the customers, but he wondered about the vendors. "What consideration should I be giving to them?" he asked himself.

He had never given much thought to his vendors before. He bought most of his products from one vendor since they carried what he needed. Even though they had been purchasing from them, Matt didn't have any real relationship with them at all. "Well, I guess I can just make myself a little more friendly to them," he thought to himself. "Why don't I share my new purpose with the delivery driver? I'll do that and ask him to hold me and the team accountable if he ever feels like we're not living by our newly defined principles," Matt said to himself.

The next time the delivery driver arrived with an order for the bakery, Matt made it a point to talk with Mark, the driver, and he shared the purpose and principles with him. "We want to make the world happy by giving moments of joy. We should always be kind, compassionate, cheerful, and clever. And for us, clever means witty, fun and creative." Matt explained. "I'm giving you permission, in fact I'm asking you, if you ever see me or anyone on our team behave in a way that doesn't align with these principles, just let me know."

"Wow, that's neat," Mark responded. "I'll let you know if something comes up." Matt and Mark continued to talk briefly before Mark had to head off to his next delivery.

One night Matt had to work late since a steam cleaning company was coming in after hours to clean the floors of the bakery. The flour dust residue and grease from the doughnut fryer had slowly accumulated and made the floors a little slippery. As the crew was steam cleaning the floor, Matt rested in his office and as he looked up at his wall calendar. He realized; he had worked the past 19 days in a row without an off day.

As the owner of a small business, it was not unusual to have to work some long hours. It was not unusual to miss an off day from time to time, but it was all starting to catch up with Matt. All the changes he had implemented with the team, and the new customer promotion were all good things, but he could feel himself starting to slow down. He was getting tired.

"That's why you need to focus on yourself sometimes," Matt whispered to himself as he sighed. "It's my own fault," he confessed. "There were a couple of days that I was only going to spend a few minutes at work, and it turned into hours. I should have just left it with Nicole and stayed home. It's not like she can't handle things when I'm not here. I know she would call if something came up." Matt sat in silence for a minute and then said to himself,

"I'm going to do better."

The next day, Matt spoke with Nicole and let her know that moving forward neither he nor she would be on the schedule for more than five days a week. If there was an emergency, they would call for help, but they would respect the other's time enough to allow them to have their day off in peace. "No more calls on off days except for emergencies," Matt and Nicole agreed.

Matt reflected on all that had transpired over the last couple of months. A smile came to his face as he thought about Nicole being his Assistant Manager, and the team meeting with their direct reports regularly. He thought about how the team members seemed to be contributing to the success of the bakery more than ever. He didn't know if it was the new purpose or just the way that Matt was slowly changing how he managed the team.

The customer loyalty program was off to a successful launch. The customers expressed a lot of excitement about the program, and they were beginning to redeem their points. So, it felt like a big win for everyone.

Matt or Nicole always made the effort to check in the deliveries to the bakery and to talk to the driver with the hope that stopping at the bakery would be one of their more pleasant stops on their delivery route.

Lastly, Matt did better at fighting the urge to be at work

when he was off. He found that he was able to better enjoy his time with his family when he wasn't always thinking about the bakery. It took some time, but it was a much-needed adjustment. The bakery had consumed him after his father had passed away. He was starting to feel like he was in over his head when he met Laura, and now things were really starting to turn around.

Chapter Four Reflection Questions

1. Matt found there was a correlation between team member satisfaction and customer satisfaction. How can team member satisfaction impact your organization?
2. How can you show appreciation to your customers without creating a loyalty program?
3. Do your business partners have permission to hold your organization accountable to its purpose and principles?
4. What steps can you take to better care for yourself?

_____

_____

_____

_____

_____

_____

_____

CHAPTER FIVE

Matt scheduled some time to meet with Laura so he wouldn't disrupt her work at the coffee shop. He asked if he could treat her to a nice lunch in repayment for all her guidance, and it would give him a chance to share the progress he had made since they last connected.

Matt and Laura met at a small farm to table diner that was just down the road from both The Corner Bakery and the Common Ground coffee shop. They sat in the booth near the corner of the diner so they could see the small nearby lake and also watch the cars as they passed.

"Laura, I just want to thank you again for your guidance and for teaching me about relational leadership. The past few months have been incredible. I'm ever so thankful for you," Matt said after the server took their order. "Oh, it's been a pleasure, Matt. Just watching your eyes light up as you've grabbed hold of the concepts of relational leadership has been exciting," Laura responded.

"Oh, it's been more than just grasping the concepts. I've put in the work, and I'm starting to see the results from it as well," he said with excitement in his voice. "That makes me so happy, Matt. I'm proud of you," Laura said with a big smile.

Matt and Laura talked and ate for quite some time as he shared the details of everything that had been implemented at the bakery since they last spoke. Laura listened intently and enjoyed hearing all the details. "There is nothing more pleasing than seeing people grow in their God given potential," Laura told Matt. As he continued to share, she couldn't help but be reminded of how Calvin would come home and share his excitement when a team member got a promotion or something new happened at work. Matt shared that same enthusiasm.

> *There is nothing more pleasing than seeing people grow in their God given potential.*

After some time, Matt paused. "I guess I've shared about everything," he said smiling. "Well, a lot has transpired in such a short time. I can hear how it's impacted you personally, as well. When we first met, you sounded like you were about to give up on the bakery," expressed Laura. "I almost was," Matt admitted as he looked down feeling a little ashamed that it had ever crossed his mind.

"You've got a team of people that are dependent on you. Not only that, but you've also got a purpose that might never be fulfilled if you and your team don't work towards it! That's your true North now. That's what you can focus on when you feel like giving up in the future. It'll help keep you firmly planted," said Laura.

"I hadn't thought of it like that Laura. I guess I just viewed the bakery as a way of earning an income. It felt good to make enough money to pay a few people along the way, but having a larger purpose has helped all of us to focus on more important things and not to get lost in a list of required tasks that generate income." Matt had a look of satisfaction about him. Not only was his belly full from eating lunch, but he had a full spirit from the experience of the past few months.

"I know the next area of relational leadership is to focus on profits," Matt commented. Laura confirmed, "Yes, that's the fourth leg of the chair Matt. Keep in mind, you'll have to focus on all four areas at once to maintain any long-term success. From time to time, one leg will require more attention than another, but they're all needed, and none can be neglected for long before things get out of balance."

"Yes, I understand," Matt responded. "I'm anxious to hear your wisdom about profits. Do you have time to share with me now?" He asked. "Of course, I'll be glad to, Matt," Laura said. She paused before speaking again. "I'm not a financial consultant or a legal expert, but what I'm about to share worked for Calvin in his business, and he and I practiced it all the time." Laura said with a smile.

"I believe it's acceptable for every organization to earn a profit, but as the leader, our job is to be a good steward of the money. Unfortunately, the leaders of some organizations appear to only be concerned about themselves. One of the most important aspects of relational leadership is serving the needs of others. Sometimes we can get caught up in the day-to-day business and forget that."

> *One of the most important aspects of relational leadership is serving the needs of others.*

"Think about it, how many pay raises do I need when my team members might have needs that are not being met? Or what if our organization prospers beyond belief, and we do nothing to help our community?"

"My philosophy has been the following:
    1. Save some profits to invest in the

company's future.

2. Save some profits to invest in the community.

3. Save some profits to invest in the team members.

4. Save some profits for other investments."

Laura paused as Matt took out his phone to take notes of what she was sharing with him. "Go ahead," he said, after he captured what was just said. "Tell me a little bit more," He requested.

"The first thing you want to do is save some of the profits to invest in the future of the business. It's like putting money in the bank for a rainy day. You'll have the money when you need it. One day, you might want to do a physical expansion of your bakery. Wouldn't it be nice to do that without having to borrow money from the bank? It takes both planning and discipline to do this. Most of the times we spend whatever comes in. We earn more, so we spend more. Setting money aside creates some margin or a buffer in our cash flow."

"The second area you want to save profit is for investing in the community. This will look different for every organization. Some companies give money to fight homelessness, others for digging wells in Africa, and still others help fund the protection of endangered animals. There are a lot of options. You'll have to determine what's a good fit for your company. I encourage you to ask yourself if the community cause you select fits the purpose and principles of your company and speaks to you in some way. Of course, you can have more than one area that you're involved with in the community. You don't have to limit yourself to just one. It's great if you can invest enough to see the impact you're making."

"Then, what most companies don't think about is supporting their own team members that might have unmet needs. It doesn't make a lot of sense to help someone across the block or on the other side of the world, and your own team members have needs. So, I like to be sure that money is designated to our team members, too. That's the third area of investing profits; setting aside money to invest in your team members."

Laura continued, "I know of one company that sets aside money for school scholarships. The investment could be spent on the team members in the form of bonuses or in the form of paid time off for special life events. Another example of this is a company that I know that sets aside money for their team members to go on trips to see where they're digging the wells in Africa. That helps the team members feel like part of the larger vision of the company. Let's face it, it also makes a memorable experience that they might not have otherwise. So, here again, it's going to look differently for each company. It's another great way to demonstrate to your team how important they are."

"The fourth and final area is saving for other investments. You have to be cautious with this, but it gives the company a chance to have some diversified income from investments outside of your company. You have to measure the risks to ensure it's realistic for your company. You want to give consideration to what would happen if the investment ends up being a flop? Could you afford to have that kind of a loss and not impact the rest of your business? So, don't jump into this area too quickly. Take calculated risks and learn as much as you can before you invest. You might want to invest in partnerships with other companies. You might even want to invest in traditional investments like mutual funds, stocks or even certificates of deposits. That's all up to you. Just be sure you have good guidance on this area."

"So, what questions do you have for me, Matt?" Laura asked. "I think you did a great job explaining it. You know me Laura, I'm going to need some time to think about it before I make any decisions," Matt responded.

As the conversation ended, Matt escorted Laura to her car as they left the diner. "Thank you again, Laura. You've been such a big help to me. Is there any way that I can ever repay you for your help?" Matt asked. "Matt, the best way you can repay me is to share what you've learned with someone else that has need of help," Laura said with a big smile.

As they went their separate ways, Matt began to think

of ways he could invest in the community and stay true to the newly defined purpose of the company; "We want to make the world happy by giving moments of joy". Just as he was thinking about the purpose, he remembered how grateful his elderly neighbor had been for all the help he had given her. "Maybe the bakery could help sponsor a home for older people or something," Matt said out loud to himself.

Matt drove to the bakery and shared the idea of helping out in the community with the team members there. They liked the idea of helping people that were sometimes overlooked and in need of help. They brainstormed practical ideas on ways they could help. It sounded like a good fit, and it also sounded like an idea the team members were willing to get behind. Since there had been so many changes at the bakery lately, Matt knew it would be important to have the support of as many team members as possible.

"Hey Nicole, thank you for being so flexible and adapting to all these changes. I appreciate you supporting all these changes and helping to implement them as well," Matt expressed. "I've enjoyed it," Nicole responded. "You know Matt, it feels like you're more engaged in the business than you were before all of these changes happened," she said. "I'll have to admit, I feel more excited about the bakery now than I ever had," he responded.

He began to review all of the changes that had taken

place as he embraced relational leadership:

"Our new purpose is: "We want to make the world happy by giving moments of joy."

"Our principles are Kind, Compassionate, Cheerful, and Clever"

"I've realigned my focus on the primary people: Team members, customers, vendors and myself. "

"And I'm beginning to focus on how I can better steward our profits: future investments in the company, investing in the community, investing in the team members, and diversifying in other areas of investments."

"That's a lot of change in a short period of time. It's a cause for a celebration!" Matt exclaimed to Nicole. He and Nicole looked at the calendar and selected an afternoon that the bakery could close early. That would allow the team time to celebrate after hours and not worry about the business. There would be food, fun and prizes. He also wanted to get something special for each team member as a reminder of the transition.

Matt knew that in time all the changes would become part of the culture of the bakery and any newly hired team members would be able to determine if the bakery culture was a "good fit" for them or not. The existing team members had to adjust along the way, but it appeared like most of the team had adapted well.

He knew that his work as leader would not end. He was committed to focusing on all four areas of relational leadership. No doubt there would be times in the future he might feel like giving up again, but with the new changes, it didn't feel like he had to carry all the weight of it alone. He was pleased with the changes and was looking forward to the future.

Chapter Five Reflection Questions

1. Proper stewardship of finances is important. On a scale of 1-5 how would you rate your financial stewardship? (1 is low and 5 is best)
2. How is your organization currently financially investing in the community?
3. Are there new or different areas of opportunities to invest in the community?
4. How is your organization currently investing in your team members financially?

_____

_____

_____

_____

_____

_____

_____

_____

CONCLUSION

You may have read this book and thought, "Relational leadership is a great idea, but I'm not a business owner, so it doesn't apply to me." I challenge you to think differently. Relational leadership is a lifestyle and not a position of employment. It's my belief that anyone can be a relational leader within their own community.

> *Relational Leadership is a lifestyle and not a position of employment.*

I believe that being a relational leader can change the environment where you are and enrich the lives of the people around you. As you may have noted in the last chapter, one of the largest components of relational leadership is serving those around you. That's how you impact your world!

A business owner or CEO may have a more direct impact on a company or organization, but you can influence your department or the team. As you walk out relational leadership principles within the context of your organization, I believe that you'll see positive change within your sphere of influence.

You may be limited by the policies and practices of the organization, but that doesn't leave you without a place to practice relational leadership. I encourage you to look at the relational leadership areas of focus and determine what level of influence you can have on your company or organization. Embrace what you can change, and don't get caught up in negativity or self-pity in the areas that are beyond your control. Remember, one of the key elements of relational leadership is serving others. So, serve with gladness.

> *A key element of relational leadership is serving others. So, serve with gladness.*

I also recognize there are several other character areas that could have been included as part of relational leadership. This book is not intended to be an exhaustive book detailing every aspect of relational leadership. My intention is to introduce the concept and add some clarity around the four primary areas. As of this writing, I have found very little information on the topic, so I thought it was important to introduce it in a thought-provoking manner.

Keep this in mind, leadership is not just a paid position. Anyone can be a leader by setting an example for others. So, lead and lead well!

> *Leadership is not a paid position.*
> *Anyone can be a leader,*
> *by setting an example for others.*

One last thought:

When I was thinking about how to approach the topic of relational leadership, I realized how far I am from being an outstanding example. Who am I to teach or try to train people about relational leadership? Relational leadership does not come naturally for me. I have to work at it. Dare I confess that I can focus much easier on tasks than I can on people? Surely, I'm not the only one. Maybe that's why this book needed to be written.

As I set out to write this book I began to reflect on past leaders in my life. I wanted to think of someone that would exemplify it best. One day it hit me! The best example that I can think of is Jesus Christ. He really is the best example of relational leadership that there is. I know some readers might be rolling your eyes right now but hear me out on this one.

You don't have to be a Christian or a follower of Christ to look at his example in scriptures and to see that he fits the position of a relational leader extremely well. Let's take a few minutes to examine his example. Let's revisit the four areas that relational leaders focus on and see how well Christ fulfills the role. In short, if we emulate him, we are emulating a true relational leader. Once again, the four areas of focus are: Purpose, Principles, People, and Profits.

Purpose

From scripture, it's clear that Christ came and understood his purpose from an early age. The Bible tells of an account in Luke chapter two that at the age of twelve Jesus got separated from his parents. He was with his parents for their annual trip to Jerusalem for the Passover Feast. No doubt it was a big event with lots of people as they traveled from near and far for this annual celebration. Somehow Jesus got separated from his parents as they were leaving the celebration. His parents assumed he was somewhere in the group that they were traveling with to their homeland.

At some point Jesus's parents realized he was not with their group. Can you imagine? They didn't find him for three days! They had to turn around and go back to where they had been to find him! His response? "Didn't you know that I needed to be about my heavenly Father's business?" – He knew what his purpose was. He also reiterated that same purpose again in the book of John in chapter six verse thirty-eight when he said, "I have come down from heaven not to do my will but to do the will of him who sent me."

Later in Jesus's life, the writer of Hebrews tells us in chapter twelve verse two that "for the joy set before him, he endured the cross." So, Christ's purpose is what kept him moving forward when things were at their darkest point. As relational leaders, that's why it's important that we serve a purpose much larger than ourselves. Our purpose becomes our true North; the thing that we focus on when we want clarity on making decisions or clarity on what next steps to take. We assess where we are, and we can ask ourselves, "What is the next step I can take to get closer to my purpose?"

Principles

We can see throughout the scriptures that Jesus was a man of solid principles, and he did not compromise. Just before his ministry started, he went out to the wilderness to meditate and pray. The book of Matthew chapter four tells the account where Jesus was tempted three times and all three times, he resisted by standing on principles that he believed in. His principles were rooted and grounded in the scriptures that existed in that day. He could recall those principles from memory and apply them to keep him headed towards his purpose. If our purpose is our true North, we can think of our principles as the compass that guides our pathway to that true North.

People

If you are a Bible reading person at all, you will know that Jesus's purpose was to save people from an eternity separated from God. So, he offered himself as a sacrifice for everyone regardless of race, gender, ethnic group, or economic status in life. In fact, he was so focused on people that in the book of John chapter three verse seventeen it says, he didn't come to judge the world, but to save the world.

In the Bible you can see Jesus continually helped others in need, even when it wasn't the culturally correct thing to do. From the Samaritan woman at the well in the book of John chapter four to the story about the "good Samaritan" that put the religious people to shame. Jesus didn't even follow tradition when a woman was caught in adultery. Tradition dictated she should have been stoned to death. He let her live. So, Jesus wasn't afraid to help people in their time of need, regardless of who they were. As a relational leader, we will often make a sacrifice for the greater good of moving towards our determined purpose.

It's worth pointing out that Jesus often withdrew from the crowd and spent time alone in prayer. So, like every relational leader, he spent time taking care of himself. There are plenty of statistics available that prove meditation and prayer are healthy for us. Take time to rest, refresh, and restore yourself so you can continue to be a good relational leader.

Profits

We don't really hear about financial profit in the Bible, but Jesus was a big proponent of being a good steward of his finances. There are two occasions in the book of Matthew that the question of paying taxes comes up. In Matthew twenty-two, Jesus advises to "give to Ceaser what is Ceaser's" despite the added burden the Roman tax collectors put on the people in that period of history. In the second account in Matthew seventeen, Jesus directs one of his men to open a fish's mouth, to reveal the needed tax money. So, he was obedient to the laws of the land.

Beyond paying taxes, Jesus often shared parables about the wages of workers in the fields and about the servants handling money when their master was away. One could argue a number of these are not genuinely talking about money but about spiritual principles, but it's clear Jesus often used practical things of this earth to illustrate things that were unseen. Without question, he was a proponent of being a good steward of whatever he possessed. We should do the same. What time, talent, or treasure have you been entrusted with that you could better steward to make the world a better place? Let's take simple steps toward better stewardship today.

Closing Thoughts

From these few examples, you can see that Jesus Christ is a great example of a relational leader. If you are not a follower of Christ, you can still follow his principles and see a good measure of success. The concepts are as dependable as the law of gravity. Plain and simple; they work. If you would like to be a follower of Christ, then that's another whole journey that is worth having a conversation about. Don't look for someone perfect to show you the way but look for someone who is sincere and moving in the right direction. Find someone that is already walking in the principles of relational leadership, they'll be glad to mentor you or to provide you with guidance.

If you are already a follower of Christ, then I challenge you to hone your skills as a relational leader. You might not always get it right but keep working towards it and keep sharing what you know. In the story you just read Laura had a chance to share with Matt. At the end of the story, you may have noticed when Matt asked how he could repay Laura for all her help, she challenged him to help someone else in need. Shouldn't every relational leader help others along the way? That's my challenge for you. Go and help someone in need as you journey towards your purpose.

Conclusion Review Questions
1. What areas of your life can you become a leader?
2. Do you have a mentor to help you become a better leader?
3. Who can you help mentor to become a better leader?
4. Do you have anyone that can guide you in becoming a better relational leader?

5. Now that you've finished this book, what is the next step that you should take?

_____

_____

_____

_____

_____

_____

_____

_____

_____

_____

_____

_____

_____

_____

_____

_____

_____

_____

_____

_____

ABOUT THE AUTHOR

Leonard Cochran is the Chief Engagement Officer of UpWords Unlimited, LLC. The company is focused on training relational leadership skills to emerging and existing leaders. He enjoys speaking, coaching, and training leadership skills and seeing lives transformed.

Leonard has been married to his best friend for over 35 years. He and his wife enjoy spending time with their two adult children and their spouses along with their two grandchildren.

Leonard also enjoys helping his wife in managing a 12-month restoration and recovery residential home for women. The 501c3 organization is run 100% by volunteers and there is very little cost to the women in the program. The organization is called Leahshouse.com.

If you would like to know more about Relational Leadership or contact Leonard to learn more, then follow one of the following links:

@LeonardCochran on LinkedIn and Facebook
@UpWordsUnlimited on Facebook and YouTube
UpWordsUnlimited.com